ROLLING STONES
IN CONCERT

THE ROLLING STONES IN CONCERT

Text by
LINDA MARTIN

Produced by
TED SMART AND DAVID GIBBON

COLOUR LIBRARY BOOKS

THE ROLLING STONES

stone by stone

■ MICK JAGGER

Vocals and harmonica, born Dartford, Kent; age 19; Mick is in his second year at the London School of Economics, but has no idea of economics himself. Likes money and spends it like water. Likes Chinese food, clothes, The Rolling Stones, Bo Diddley, and life in general. Underneath that mousey mop of hair lie two big blue eyes. Has been with the group from its birth.

■ BRIAN JONES

Vocals/guitar and harmonica; born in Cheltenham, moved to London two years ago. Age 19. Blonde-haired Brian smokes 60 cigarettes a day and has packed a lot of different jobs into his 19 years including coal lorry driving; assistant in an architect's office; playing in a jazz band and a year's hitch-hiking on the Continent. Fascinated by the railways; wants to be President of the Dr. Beeching Fan Club.

■ KEITH RICHARD

Guitar. Black haired Keith was born in Dartford 19 years ago; worked in a post office. Has one romance in his life - his guitar! Would like a house-boat on the Thames; collects Chuck Berry and Jimmy Reed records.

■ BILL WYMAN

Bass guitar/vocals. Hollow cheeked Bill is 21 and is often called "The Ghost" due to his pale complexion. Interested in poetry; books; food. Another Chuck Berry fan, Bill has dark hair and hails from Beckenham, Kent.

■ CHARLIE WATTS

Drums. 21-year-old Charlie is the "Beau Brummell" of the group. Has over 100 pocket handkerchiefs. "Charlie Boy", as he is called, lives in Wembley, has spent the last year between an advertising agency and The Rolling Stones.

This press release was issued by Eric Easton and Andrew Loog Oldham in 1963, shortly before the Rolling Stones became famous. Andrew Oldham first saw the Stones at the famous Crawdaddy Club in Richmond, and one look was enough—he and his boss, Eric Easton, immediately signed them to an exclusive management contract. Oldham was not slow to realise the potential value of the Stones' 'bad boy' image either, and the neat and tidy houndstooth jackets and smart black trousers right were quickly discarded. Top row, left to right: *Bill Wyman, Keith Richards, Brian Jones;* bottom row: *Mick Jagger, Charlie Watts.*

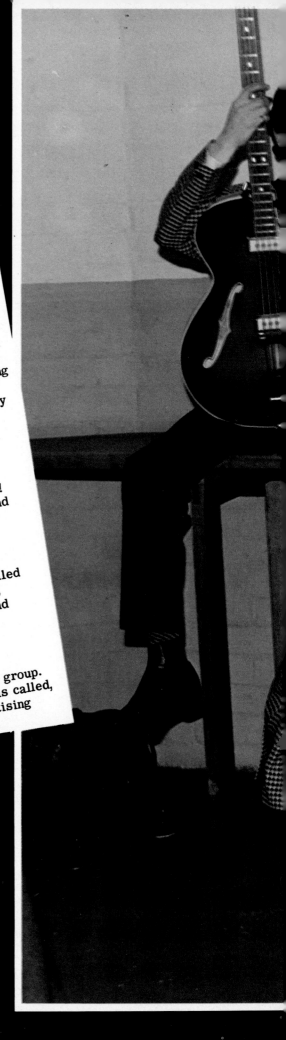

TOURS

1963   September / October / November: Britain.

1964   January/February/March: Britain.
June: North America.
August: Britain (including one of the first open-air rock concerts, at Longleat House).
September/October: Britain.
October/November: North America.

1965   January/February: Australia, New Zealand, Singapore and Hong Kong.
March: Britain.
March/April: Scandinavia.
April: Germany and France.
April/May: North America.
June: Scotland.
June: Scandinavia.
September: Germany and Austria.
September/October: Britain.
October / November / December: North America.

1966   February/March: Australia and New Zealand.
March/April: Holland, Belgium, France, Sweden and Denmark.
June/July: North America.
September/October: Britain.

1967   March/April: Sweden, Germany, Austria, Italy, France, Poland, Switzerland, Holland and Greece.

1969   November: North America.

1970   September/October: Finland, Sweden, Denmark, Germany, France, Austria, Italy and Holland.

1971   March: Britain.

1972   June/July: North America.

1973   January/February: Hawaii, Hong Kong, New Zealand and Australia.
September/October: Austria, Germany, England, Scotland, Switzerland, Denmark, Sweden, Holland and Belgium.

1975   June/July/August: The Americas (South American dates were subsequently cancelled).

1976   April/May/June: Germany, Belgium, Scotland, England, Holland, France, Spain, Switzerland, Yugoslavia and Austria.

1977   March: North America.

1978   June/July: North America.

1981   September/October/November/December: North America.

DISCOGRAPHY

Singles and EPs *(US titles in italics)*

Title	Label	Date
Come On/I Want To Be Loved	Decca	June 1963
I Wanna Be Your Man/Stoned	Decca	November 1963
The Rolling Stones EP: Bye Bye Johnny/Money/You Better Move On/Poison Ivy	Decca	January 1964
Not Fade Away/Little By Little	Decca	February 1964
Not Fade Away/I Wanna Be Your Man	London	March 1964
It's All Over Now/Good Times, Bad Times	Decca	June 1964
Tell Me/I Just Want To Make Love To You	London	June 1964
It's All Over Now/Good Times, Bad Times	London	July 1964
Five By Five EP: If You Need Me/Empty Heart/2120 South Michigan Avenue/Confessin' The Blues/Around and Around	Decca	August 1964
Time Is On My Side/Congratulations	London	September 1964
Little Red Rooster/Off The Hook	Decca	November 1964
Heart of Stone/What A Shame	London	December 1964
The Last Time/Play With Fire	Decca	February 1965
The Last Time/Play With Fire	London	March 1965
(I Can't Get No) Satisfaction/The Under Assistant West Coast Promotion Man	London	May 1965
Got Live If You Want It! EP: We Want The Stones/Everybody Needs Somebody To Love/Pain In My Heart/(Get Your Kicks On) Route 66/I'm Moving On/I'm Alright	Decca	June 1965
(I Can't Get No) Satisfaction/The Spider And The Fly	Decca	August 1965
Get Off Of My Cloud/I'm Free	London	September 1965
Get Off Of My Cloud/The Singer Not The Song	Decca	October 1965
As Tears Go By/Gotta Get Away	London	December 1965
19th Nervous Breakdown/Sad Day	London	February 1966
19th Nervous Breakdown/As Tears Go By	Decca	February 1966
Paint It Black/Stupid Girl	London	April 1966
Paint It Black/Long, Long While	Decca	May 1966
Mother's Little Helper/Lady Jane	London	June 1966
Have You Seen Your Mother, Baby, Standing In The Shadow?/Who's Driving Your Plane	Decca	September 1966
Have You Seen Your Mother, Baby, Standing In The Shadow?/Who's Driving Your Plane	London	September 1966
Let's Spend The Night Together/Ruby Tuesday	London	January 1967
Let's Spend The Night Together/Ruby Tuesday	Decca	January 1967
We Love You/Dandelion	London	August 1967
We Love You/Dandelion	Decca	August 1967
She's A Rainbow/2000 Light Years From Home	London	November 1967
In Another Land/The Lantern	London	December 1967
Jumpin' Jack Flash/Child Of The Moon	Decca	May 1968
Jumpin' Jack Flash/Child Of The Moon	London	May 1968
Street Fighting Man/No Expectations	London	August 1968
Honky Tonk Women/You Can't Always Get What You Want	Decca	July 1969
Honky Tonk Women/You Can't Always Get What You Want	London	July 1969
Street Fighting Man/Surprise, Surprise	Decca	July 1970
Brown Sugar/Bitch/Let It Rock	Rolling Stones Records	April 1971
Brown Sugar/Bitch	RSR	May 1971
Wild Horses/Sway	RSR	June 1971
Tumbling Dice/Sweet Black Angel	RSR	April 1972
Tumbling Dice/Sweet Black Angel	RSR	April 1972
Happy/All Down The Line	RSR	June 1972
Angie/Silver Train	RSR	August 1973
Angie/Silver Train	RSR	August 1973
Doo Doo Doo Doo (Heartbreaker)/Dancing With Mr D	RSR	December 1973
It's Only Rock 'n' Roll/Through The Lonely Night	RSR	July 1974

It's Only Rock 'n' Roll/ Through The Lonely Night	RSR	July 1974
Ain't Too Proud To Beg/ Dance Little Sister	RSR	October 1974
I Don't Know Why/Try A Little Harder	Decca	May 1975
I Don't Know Why/Try A Little Harder	ABKCO	May 1975
Out Of Time/Jiving Sister Fanny	Decca	September 1975
Out Of Time/Jiving Sister Fanny	ABKCO	September 1975
Fool To Cry/Hot Stuff	Rolling Stones Records	April 1976
Fool To Cry/Crazy Mama	RSR	April 1976
Miss You/Girl With The Faraway Eyes	EMI	May 1976
Miss You/Girl With The Faraway Eyes	Rolling Stones Records	June 1976
Respectable/When The Whip Comes Down	EMI	September 1978
Beast Of Burden/When The Whip Comes Down	Rolling Stones Records	November 1978
Emotional Rescue/Down The Hole	RSR	June 1980
Emotional Rescue/Down The Hole	RSR	June 1980
Start Me Up/No Use In Crying	RSR	September 1981
Start Me Up/No Use In Crying	RSR	September 1981
Waiting On A Friend/Little T & A	RSR	December 1981
Waiting On A Friend/Little T & A	RSR	December 1981

Albums (US titles in italics)—Does not include compilation albums.

The Rolling Stones (Decca, April 1964) Route 66, I Just Want To Make Love To You, Honest I Do, I Need You Baby, Now I've Got A Witness, Little By Little, I'm A King Bee, Carol, Tell Me, Can I Get A Witness, You Can Make It If You Try, Walking The Dog.

England's Newest Hit Makers—The Rolling Stones (London, May 1964) Not Fade Away, Route 66, I Just Want To Make Love To You, Honest I Do, Now I've Got A Witness, Little By Little, I'm A King Bee, Carol, Tell Me, Can I Get A Witness, You Can Make It If You Try, Walking The Dog.

12 x 5 (London, October 1964) Around And Around, Confessin' The Blues, Empty Heart, Time Is On My Side, Good Times, Bad Times, It's All Over Now, 2120 South Michigan Avenue, Under The Boardwalk, Congratulations, Grown Up Wrong, If You Need Me, Susie Q.

The Rolling Stones No 2 (Decca, January 1965) Everybody Needs Somebody To Love, Down Home Girl, You Can't Catch Me, Time Is On My Side, What A Shame, Grown Up Wrong, Down The Road Apiece, Under The Boardwalk, I Can't Be Satisfied, Pain In My Heart, Off The Hook, Susie Q.

The Rolling Stones, Now (London, February 1965) Everybody Needs Somebody To Love, Down Home Girl, You Can't Catch Me, Heart Of Stone, What A Shame, I Need You Baby, Down The Road Apiece, Off The Hook, Pain In My Heart, Oh Baby, Little Red Rooster, Surprise, Surprise.

Out Of Our Heads (London, July 1965) Mercy Mercy, Hitch Hike, The Last Time, That's How Strong My Love Is, Good Times, I'm Alright, (I Can't Get No) Satisfaction, Cry To Me, The Under Assistant West Coast Promotion Man, Play With Fire, The Spider And The Fly, One More Try.

Out Of Our Heads (Decca, September 1965) She Said Yeah, Mercy Mercy, Hitch Hike, That's How Strong My Love Is, Good Times, Gotta Get Away, Talkin' 'Bout You, Cry To Me, Oh Baby, Heart Of Stone, The Under Assistant West Coast Promotion Man, I'm Free.

December's Children (London, November 1965) She Said Yeah, Talkin' 'Bout You, You Better Move On, Look What You've Done, The Singer Not The Song, Route 66, Get Off Of My Cloud, I'm Free, As Tears Go By, Gotta Get Away, Blue Turns To Grey, I'm Moving On.

Aftermath (Decca, April 1966) Mother's Little Helper, Stupid Girl, Lady Jane, Under My Thumb, Doncha Bother Me, Goin' Home, Flight 505, High And Dry, Out Of Time, It's Not Easy, I Am Waiting, Take It Or Leave It, Think, What To Do.

Aftermath (London, June 1966) Paint It Black, Stupid Girl, Lady Jane, Under My Thumb, Doncha Bother Me, Think, Flight 505, High And Dry, It's Not Easy, I Am Waiting, Goin' Home.

Got Live If You Want It! (London, November 1966) Under My Thumb, Get Off Of My Cloud, Lady Jane, Not Fade Away, I've Been Loving You Too Long, Fortune Teller, The Last Time, 19th Nervous Breakdown, Time Is On My Side, I'm Alright, Have You Seen Your Mother, Baby, Standing In The Shadow?, (I Can't Get No) Satisfaction.

Between The Buttons (Decca, January 1967) Yesterday's Papers, My Obsession, Back Street Girl, Connection, She Smiled Sweetly, Cool, Calm And Collected, All Sold Out, Please Go Home, Who's Been Sleeping Here, Complicated, Miss Amanda Jones, Something Happened To Me Yesterday.

Between The Buttons (London, January 1967) Let's Spend The Night Together, Yesterday's Papers, Ruby Tuesday, Connection, She Smiled Sweetly, Cool, Calm And Collected, All Sold Out, My Obsession, Who's Been Sleeping Here, Complicated, Miss Amanda Jones, Something Happened To Me Yesterday.

DISCOGRAPHY

Flowers (_London, June 1967_) Ruby Tuesday, Have You Seen Your Mother, Baby, Standing In The Shadow?, Let's Spend The Night Together, Lady Jane, Out Of Time, My Girl, Back Street Girl, Please Go Home, Mother's Little Helper, Take It Or Leave It, Ride On Baby, Sittin' On A Fence.

Their Satanic Majesties Request (_London, November 1967;_ Decca, December 1967) Sing This All Together, Citadel, In Another Land, 2000 Man, Sing This All Together (See What Happens), She's A Rainbow, The Lantern, Gomper, 2000 Light Years From Home, On With The Show.

Beggar's Banquet (_London, November 1968;_ Decca, December 1968) Sympathy For The Devil, No Expectations, Dear Doctor, Parachute Woman, Jig-Saw Puzzle, Street Fighting Man, Prodigal Son, Stray Cat Blues, Factory Girl, Salt Of The Earth.

Let It Bleed (_London, November 1969;_ Decca, December 1969) Gimme Shelter, Love In Vain, Country Honk, Live With Me, Let It Bleed, Midnight Rambler, You Got The Silver, Monkey Man, You Can't Always Get What You Want.

Get Yer Ya-Ya's Out! (_London, September 1970;_ Decca, September 1970) Jumpin' Jack Flash, Carol, Stray Cat Blues, Love In Vain, Midnight Rambler, Sympathy For The Devil, Live With Me, Little Queenie, Honky Tonk Women, Street Fighting Man.

The following albums were released simultaneously in the US and UK.

Sticky Fingers (Rolling Stones Records, April 1971) Brown Sugar, Sway, Wild Horses, Can't You Hear Me Knocking, You Gotta Move, Bitch, I Got The Blues, Sister Morphine, Dead Flowers, Moonlight Mile.

Exile On Main Street (Rolling Stones Records, May 1972) **Double Album** Rocks Off, Rip This Joint, Shake Your Hips, Casino Boogie, Tumbling Dice, Sweet Virginia, Torn And Frayed, Sweet Black Angel, Loving Cup, Happy, Turd On The Run, Ventilator Blues, I Just Want To See His Face, Let It Loose, All Down The Line, Stop Breaking Down, Shine A Light, Soul Survivor.

Goats Head Soup (Rolling Stones Records, August 1973) Dancing With Mr D, 100 Years Ago, Coming Down Again, Doo Doo Doo Doo (Heartbreaker), Angie, Silver Train, Hide Your Love, Winter, Can You Hear The Music, Star Star.

It's Only Rock 'n' Roll (Rolling Stones Records, October 1974) If You Can't Rock Me, Ain't Too Proud To Beg, It's Only Rock 'n' Roll, Till The Next Goodbye, Time Waits For No One, Luxury, Dance Little Sister, If You Really Want To Be My Friend, Short And Curlies, Fingerprint File.

Black And Blue (Rolling Stones Records, April 1976) Hot Stuff, Hand Of Fate, Cherry Oh Baby, Memory Motel, Hey Negrita, Melody, Fool To Cry, Crazy Mama.

Love You Live (Rolling Stones Records, September 1977) **Double Album** Excerpt From Fanfare For The Common Man, Honky Tonk Women, If You Can't Rock Me, Get Off Of My Cloud, Happy, Hot Stuff, Star Star, Tumbling Dice, Fingerprint File, You Gotta Move, You Can't Always Get What You Want, Mannish Boy, Crackin' Up, Little Red Rooster, Around And Around, It's Only Rock 'n' Roll, Brown Sugar, Jumpin' Jack Flash, Sympathy For The Devil.

Some Girls (Rolling Stones Records, June 1978) Miss You, When The Whip Comes Down, Imagination, Some Girls, Lies, Far Away Eyes, Respectable, Before They Make Me Run, Beast Of Burden, Shattered.

Emotional Rescue (Rolling Stones Records, June 1980) Dance, Summer Romance, Send It To Me, Let Me Go, Indian Girl, Where The Boys Go, Down The Hole, Emotional Rescue, She's So Cold, All About You.

Tattoo You (Rolling Stones Records, September 1981) Start Me Up, Hang Fire, Slave, Little T & A, Black Limousine, Neighbours, Worried About You, Tops, Heaven, No Use In Crying, Waiting On A Friend.

**Unlike Lennon and McCartney, Jagger and Richards are not associated with creative songwriting; yet Jagger and Richards have written an enormous number of rock and roll classics, like** (I Can't Get No) Satisfaction, Get Off Of My Cloud, Jumpin' Jack Flash **and** Brown Sugar. They were encouraged to write their own material by Lennon and McCartney themselves, and their original efforts were farmed out to other artists —The Last Time was their first self-penned 'A' side. The famous 'Nanker-Phelge' name appeared on many of the group's earlier compositions: Phelge being the surname of a friend, and Nanker the name they gave to their habit of pulling faces!

COME ON

Dick Taylor, Mick Jagger, and two friends, Allen Etherington and Bob Beckwith, had formed a group called Little Boy Blue and the Blue Boys, and before long Keith Richards was invited to join them.

Meanwhile, Brian Jones was advertising for a band. Disillusioned by the lack of opportunity for his kind of music in his home town of Cheltenham, he had moved to London with the idea of forming an R & B band. He contacted Alexis Korner who, at the time, fronted one of the only authentic blues bands around, and who he had met briefly in Cheltenham. Korner

It seems hard to believe these days, but the general appearance of the Rolling Stones, and the length of their hair, caused a public outcry and prompted headlines like 'Would You Let Your Daughter Go With A Rolling Stone?' (Melody Maker, 1964).

To howls of anguish and protest from the 'Establishment', the Rolling Stones gathered fame and fortune in the early 1960's. Nearly twenty years on, they practically *are* the 'Establishment', playing to a whole new generation of fans.

The Rolling Stones' story began way back in 1950, when Keith Richards met Mick Jagger at Maypole County Primary School, Dartford, at the age of seven. They were not to meet again until 1960 when they came across each other on a

train—Keith Richards travelling to Sidcup Art School and Mick Jagger on his way to the London School of Economics. They chatted about the rhythm and blues (R & B) import albums Jagger was carrying, found they had a mutual friend, Dick Taylor, who later went on to form the Pretty Things, and discovered they had a great deal in common, particularly their love of the blues.

invited him to play with his band, Blues Incorporated, occasionally, while Jones looked for his own band. Through his advertisement in *Jazz News*, Jones met pianist, Ian Stewart, and guitarist Geoff Bradford. They frequented the Ealing Blues Club, where Alexis Korner's Blues Incorporated held a residency, and it was there during a 'jam' session that Brian Jones met Keith Richards and Mick Jagger. The three of them moved into a flat together, just off the Fulham Road.

The first half of 1962 saw them toying with the name 'the Rollin' Stones'—the title of a song by one of the great blues artists, Muddy Waters—and rehearsing whenever and wherever possible. They had acquired a drummer, Tony Chapman, and Dick Taylor and Ian Stewart completed the line-up. Times were hard for aspiring R & B bands, though, and the lack of money and engagements persuaded Dick Taylor to leave for a more promising future at the Royal College of Art. Just a short time later, the Rollin' Stones played their first engagement, deputising for Blues Incorporated at the Marquee Club (then in Oxford Street) on 12 July 1962.

By the end of that year, they had auditioned and taken on Bill Wyman as bass player (it has been suggested that he was valued rather more for his impressive amplifier than for his playing at that time!) and Charlie Watts (late of Blues Incorporated) had been approached to replace Tony Chapman, whose job as travelling salesman kept him away from more rehearsals than he attended. In January 1963, Watts finally agreed to join the Rolling Stones. Thus, at the start of the year, the group consisted of Mick Jagger (vocals), Bill Wyman (bass guitar), Keith Richards and Brian Jones (guitars), Charlie Watts (drums) and Ian Stewart (piano). (Ian Stewart—the sixth Stone—was eventually to drop away from the group,

NOT FADE AWAY

By the beginning of 1964, the Stones were rivalling the Beatles when it came to 'Scream Power'. As Keith Richards said: 'They (the fans) couldn't hear the music. We couldn't hear ourselves for years. It was impossible to play as a band on stage.' One place they could be heard was in the studio, rehearsing for TV's Ready, Steady, Go! right.

playing up to—an approach which certainly paid off.

Suddenly the Stones were news. A major tour with the Everly Brothers and Bo Diddley took them all over the country from the end of September to the beginning of November, and three days before the end of the tour their next single, *I Wanna Be Your Man*, was released. The Stones had continued to appear in the London clubs before they started their tour, and were popular with local audiences. However, they knew that they would have to find good material to record to become a major attraction. The follow-up to *Come On* was a Lennon/McCartney number, and, as such, its success was almost pre-determined. It made the Top Ten.

1964 commenced with their first tour as top of the bill, supported by the Ronettes. To coincide with the tour, an EP featuring *You Better Move On*, *Money, Poison Ivy*, and *Bye Bye Johnny* was released on 17 January, immediately entering the singles charts at Number 28. Rave reviews of the tour, plus the release of *Not Fade Away* just a month after the EP, ensured that the Stones were here to stay. The Beatles had registered with all

guesting occasionally on tour and in the recording studio.)

Their first experiment in the recording studios resulted in tapes of four of the R & B standards: *I Want To Be Loved, Roadrunner, Honey* and *Diddley Diddley Daddy*, and a Jimmy Reed song, *Bright Lights, Big City*.

Unfortunately, they couldn't find a label to release the tapes. Undeterred, the Stones aimed for, and won, a residency at one of the most important R & B venues in London—the Crawdaddy Club at the Station Hotel, Richmond-on-Thames. Here they caught the eye of celebrities like the Beatles, and it was here, on 28 April 1963, that Andrew Loog

Oldham first saw them. The next week he signed the Rolling Stones to an exclusive management contract.

Just six weeks later, the Stones had a recording contract with Decca, a new single, *Come On*, and a spot on TV's Thank Your Lucky Stars to promote it.

The first television appearance by the Rolling Stones upset many viewers— even though the Stones themselves felt that they were 'selling-out' by wearing neat little uniforms of houndstooth-check jackets and dark trousers! Surprised by the adverse reaction to his protégés, Andrew Oldham, who had suggested these outfits, decided that the Stones' 'neanderthal' image was worth age groups—the rebellious Rolling Stones were the voice of the teenager.

Their 'wild' appearance prompted one disapproving parent to write to a national newspaper asking: 'Is there any Member of Parliament with the courage to introduce a Bill (into the House of Commons) compelling boys to have their hair cut?' (*Daily Mirror, Readers' Letters*); and the President of the National Federation of Hairdressers offered a free haircut to the next Number One group or soloist in the pop charts, stating: 'The Rolling Stones are the worst. One of them looks as if he has got a feather duster on his head.' Judith Simons of the *Daily Express* wrote: 'They look like boys whom any self-respecting mum would lock in the bathroom! But the Rolling Stones—five

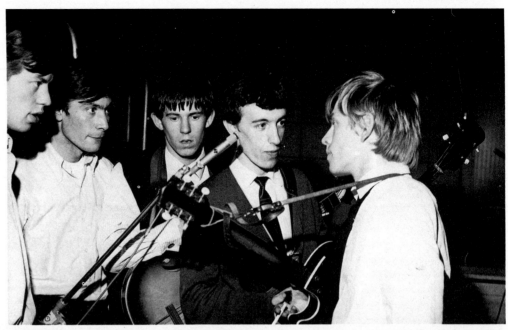

PLAY WITH FIRE

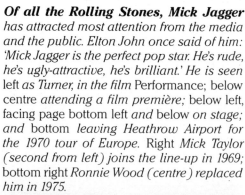

tough young London-based music makers with doorstep mouths, pallid cheeks, and unkempt hair are not worried what mums think!' This was just the sort of publicity that Andrew Oldham wanted—after all, it kept them in the public eye!

'64 was an eventful year. Kicking off with their tour in January, they appeared at the Empire Pool, Wembley, twice in April—once for the Ready Steady Go Mod Ball, and again for the *New Musical Express* Pollwinners' Concert which was televised in May. They guested on BBC TV's Juke Box Jury, toured America for the first and second time, and met their heroes, Chuck Berry, Muddy Waters and Willie Dixon, at a recording session in Chess Studios, Chicago. They were banned from future appearances on the Ed Sullivan Show after their performance sparked off hysteria in the studio

audience; and riots and screaming, stampeding fans followed them all over Europe. The Stones' live performances were seldom heard—the audience went berserk as soon as they stepped onstage. The fans had an unusual way of showing their devotion too: bottles, shoes, iron bolts and even chairs were hurled onto the stage; theatre seats were destroyed, equipment stolen and smashed; and outside the scenes were even wilder! Police had to use tear gas and water cannons to control some crowds and on several occasions the Stones themselves

EVERYBODY NEEDS SOMEBODY TO LOVE

were in fear of their lives — like the time when thousands of fans threw themselves at their car, cracking the roof and practically crushing the occupants. In between tours, however, they managed to develop their recording career, with songs like *It's All Over Now* and *Little Red Rooster*.

Yet another tour started 1965 for the Rolling Stones. This time it was Ireland. Within a fortnight they were off to Australia, and during that year they visited Scandinavia, North America and Germany twice, and France and Austria once. Between tours they recorded, and Jagger and Richards started to write their own songs, the first of which was a composition called *The Last Time*. This was the beginning of a long line of increasingly anarchic singles with titles

In 1971, Mick Jagger married the beautiful Bianca. They are seen far right *during the ceremony;* right *on honeymoon in Venice;* top right *at the opening of* Josephine *in Paris;* above *at Studio 54, New York; and* left *in 1977 after rumours of a divorce.*

like *(I Can't Get No) Satisfaction, 19th Nervous Breakdown* and *Get Off Of My Cloud.*

They found time to scandalise the public too. An incident in Stratford, London, when they were accused of insulting behaviour after urinating against the wall of a service station, ensured the furtherance of their 'outrageous' image.

That year saw the emergence of Allen Klein who was appointed as business manager for both the Rolling Stones and

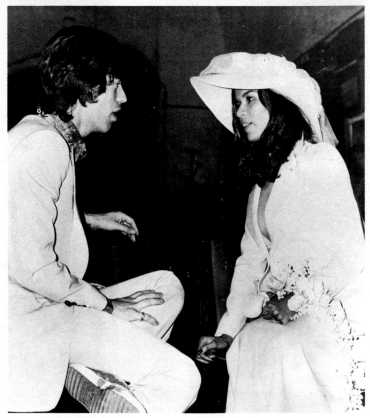

LITTLE RED ROOSTER

failing to represent their best interests and for depriving them of royalties. They eventually settled their differences in May 1972.

The frantic pace continued, even though the Stones had decided to cut out performances in dance halls (more for safety than for any other reason). They visited Australia again in February 1966, and toured five European countries in ten days in March/April. Later that year, they made their fifth North American tour, and their last British tour for over four

for their personal manager, Andrew Oldham. Klein was eventually dismissed in 1970, the Stones' partnership with Oldham having been dissolved in 1967, and Jimmy Miller having replaced him as producer of the Stones' records. Both Oldham and Klein were sued by the Rolling Stones in 1971 for allegedly

One of the Rolling Stones' first 'fan' *letters read as follows: 'The whole lot of you should be given a good bath and then all that hair should be cut off.'*

years, with the Yardbirds and Ike and Tina Turner. Allen Klein purchased the film rights of *Only Lovers Left Alive* — the group were to make their acting début and would receive a handsome $1 million for the privilege. The film, based on a novel of the same title, dealt with the imaginary conquest of England by its rebellious youth. Filming commenced in October at MGM's Boreham Wood studios, but the project was never completed.

Their hit singles that year included *Paint It Black*, which was released in May, and *Have You Seen Your Mother, Baby, Standing In The Shadow?*, which

BEGGAR'S BANQUET

'The Rolling Stones always have been and always will be not so much a group but more a way of life. A way of life still relating with each change in the world today. As the years pass and Richmond to many is but a faint echo of harmonicas in the distance from the back of a pub, disturbing the window box couples who sit to enjoy their every evening routine of the lowering of the human mind by mass communication. But to others Richmond was the seed of a group called the Rolling Stones, who since those early days of 1963 have become one of the biggest

To promote their LP, **Beggar's Banquet,** *the Stones held a 'Beggar's Banquet', complete with serving wenches, to which a number of journalists and television people were invited. The Banquet, held in December 1968, was rounded off with a custard pie battle.*

they promoted by dressing up in drag for the press advertisements. It was dressing up of a different kind that caused storms of protest to howl around Brian Jones—his appearance as a Nazi, his foot crushing a doll, which was meant to be an anti-fascist demonstration, was somehow misconstrued by almost everyone. Over the next couple of years, Jones himself was to be crushed by the pressure of being a Rolling Stone.

In four years, the Stones had risen from an obscure, blues-orientated, club-playing band to, in the words of the biography issued by Decca Records, 'a way of life':

WE LOVE YOU

pack into halls and stadiums and the millions who see them every year. In addition through the song writing talents of Mick Jagger and Keith Richards, the group has been able to amplify their potential even further than it seemed possible earlier by becoming a self-contained entity of expression, relating to one and all because Mick, Charlie, Bill, Keith and Brian on stage, on record, in song, relate to today. The girl or boy who watches them or listens to a record relates, therefore completing a chemistry that makes the Rolling Stones

the act they are. They communicate in the realisation that entertainment is both relative and a form of escapism from the 8.31 and the book of luncheon vouchers. 'The Rolling Stones, apart from the single hits of *Satisfaction, The Last Time, Paint It Black, Get Off Of My Cloud, Have You Seen Your Mother, Baby, Not Fade Away,* and the countless others, have also helped in the revolutionary movement in the world of albums, which we humbly believe in the years to come will be looked upon, as will those albums by the other top acts of today, as the guide and Bible to the world in which we live today to those who will live tomorrow. To learn about the early days of our religions we waited for Moses to descend from Mount Sinai with the two tablets which made up the ten commandments. We look to Shakespeare and Dickens and Chaucer for accounts of other times in our history, and we feel that tomorrow we will on many occasions look to the gramophone record of the Rolling Stones and the other contemporaries of today who act as a mirror of today's mind, action and happenings, for albums today are not just twelve songs but twelve stories.'

group attractions throughout the world, and have received over twenty gold records for world sales of their albums and singles, and have topped charts and packed concerts in every major country in the world.

'Their success could be attributed to many things, but regardless of changes, both outwardly and inwardly, the five Rolling Stones have been through over the past four years, the reason is still the same.

'Seeing is believing, and the pure excitement that attracted the earlier followers to the "uncommercial sound" of the Stones R & B at Richmond or Eel Pie Island, or any other sanctuary for the followers of that movement, is the same as the twenty or thirty thousand who

SYMPATHY FOR THE DEVIL

Decca's Publicity Department obviously took themselves — and the Rolling Stones — very seriously!

The Stones' most controversial record, *Let's Spend the Night Together*, was released in January 1967, and they were booked to promote it on the Ed Sullivan Show in New York — contrary to Sullivan's initial reaction to the Stones in 1964, when they had been banned from appearing on his show again. The anticipated fury of the Establishment forced Sullivan to insist that Mick Jagger substitute the words 'some time' for 'the night', which he eventually agreed to do, although he later held that he just mumbled the words. The programme went ahead, giving the

The Stones on film: during the recording of Sympathy For The Devil, this page *and* opposite page top left; *and with assorted friends, including members of The Who, Eric Clapton, John Lennon and Yoko Ono, for the still-unscreened Rock and Roll Circus left.*

group and their record a valuable plug — as many radio stations in America had refused to play it! Coupled with this was an incident on British television which the Press blew out of all proportion. The furore was caused by the refusal of the Rolling Stones to ride the carousel (revolving stage) on the popular Sunday Night At The London Palladium show — their view was that one performance on a 'family show' did

SHE'S A RAINBOW

not mean that they had become family—therefore respectable—entertainers. But by far the most momentous incident of 1967 was the raid by West Sussex police officers on Redlands—the home of Keith Richards—which resulted in the charging of both Richards and Mick Jagger for drug offences.

Jagger's offence was trifling—he was accused of possessing four tablets containing methyl amphetamine hydrochloride and amphetamine sulphate, a benzedrine type of stimulant. Richards' offence, on the other hand, was somewhat more serious in that he had allowed his premises to be used for the purpose of smoking cannabis resin. (A third defendant, Robert Fraser, was charged with, and found guilty of, possessing heroin and methyl amphetamine hydrochloride).

The ladies in Mick Jagger's life have been a constant source of interest to the Press and public alike. He is pictured with ex-wife Bianca opposite page; *and with girlfriend, top model Jerry Hall* this page, *with whom he has lived since 1977.*

The media made an enormous amount of fuss—it was the first incident of its kind, and just the sort of thing they'd been waiting for. Adding a touch more spice to the case was the story of the naked girl wrapped in a fur rug, discovered by the police during the raid. It was reported that from time to time she dropped the rug...!

Jagger and Richards both pleaded 'not guilty' to the charges. Jagger maintained that he had bought the pills in Italy, where it was quite legal to do so, and that he had not realised it was illegal to bring them into Britain without a prescription. In fact, his doctor testified

that Jagger had telephoned him on his return to check whether it was safe to use the pills. The doctor had confirmed that it was, provided they were not used regularly, and later at the trial he stated that he would have prescribed similar tablets, had Jagger not already bought them.

Strangely, the judge directed the jury that this evidence was no defence for Jagger, and they passed a verdict of 'guilty' on the defendant. He was remanded in custody until after Keith Richards' trial, and for the next few days he travelled between the local prison and the courthouse actually *handcuffed* to warders.

As expected, Richards was also found guilty. What was not expected, though, was the severity of their sentences— Jagger was given three months' imprisonment and Richards was sentenced to a year's imprisonment. After the first stunned silence, the rock world and, surprisingly, a great many influential people and members of the public, reacted strongly against such harsh punishment. An advertisement was taken out by The Who and appeared in an evening paper, criticising the sentences and accusing the court of treating Jagger and Richards as scapegoats for the drug problem. This reaction from members of the pop world was understandable, but Jagger also received support from an entirely

MIDNIGHT RAMBLER

and suspected them of decadence. In conclusion, the editorial declared a suspicion that Jagger had received a more severe sentence than would have been afforded a completely anonymous young man.

The *Melody Maker* had this to say about the case and resultant publicity:

'Because the case has aroused public interest to a large degree, many national newspapers have passed comment. The

The Stones toured Europe with Billy Preston during the latter part of 1973—they are seen these pages *and* overleaf *in Rotterdam.*

different quarter—the Editor of *The Times*, Mr William Rees-Mogg.

An editorial under the heading 'Who Breaks a Butterfly on a Wheel' appeared in the 1 July 1967 edition of *The Times*. The editorial pointed out that the offence was one of a technical nature which any citizen might unwittingly commit. It asked if the sentencing might have been less severe if the defendant had been a promising undergraduate, and whether—guilty or not—it was necessary to display Jagger handcuffed. It hinted that Jagger was treated thus because he *was* Mick Jagger; that some people agreed 'he had got what was coming to him'. It was suggested that these people resented the anarchic quality of the Rolling Stones' performances, disliked their songs and their influence on teenagers,

(I CAN'T GET NO) SATISFACTION

Melody Maker has read them all and we find ourselves, a little surprisingly, handing not one flower but a large bouquet to *The Times.* For last Saturday, *The Times* ran a leader on the Jagger case. It was objective, informed and fair. Thankfully it lacked hysteria...The *Melody Maker,* unasked by the Rolling Stones, thanks *The Times.* The *Melody Maker* bows to *The Times.* The *Melody Maker* has a message for *The Times*: KEEP SWINGING!'

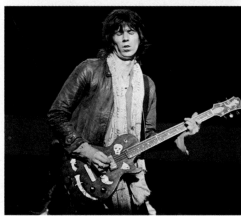

Mick Jagger and Keith Richards on stage *at the Avetoire, Paris, in 1976.*

It has been suggested that the interest of the media might have influenced the appeal hearing held on 31 July, at which Richards' conviction was quashed, and Jagger was given a conditional discharge.

HONKY TONK WOMEN

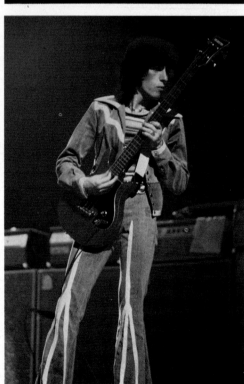

In contrast with many of their contemporaries, the Rolling Stones have always been a visual group, as opposed to a recording group. As Keith Richards said: 'Our scene is the concerts and many of our records were roughly made on purpose. Our sort of scene is to have a really good time with the audience.' Overleaf Mick Jagger finds a novel way to cool down!

TUMBLING DICE

The rumpus surrounding the trial, subsequent conviction and appeal, rather overshadowed the arrest on similar charges of another member of the group, Brian Jones. Like Jagger and Richards, he was found guilty, sentenced to nine months' imprisonment, appealed, and was set free upon payment of a £1,000 fine and three years' probation. Unlike Jagger and Richards, however, the strain and pressure of his life style, which had already resulted in one stay in hospital that year, took its toll and he was rushed into hospital again just after his appeal hearing in December,

suffering from nervous exhaustion.

The hits kept on coming, although both the single *We Love You*, released after the Jagger/Richards appeal hearing, with guest harmonies by Paul McCartney and John Lennon, and the LP *Their Satanic Majesties Request*, released in December 1967, were, to many, disappointing. *Their Satanic Majesties Request* was the Stones' first venture into the wave of psychedelic music—it would be their last. It was during the recording of this LP that

'Yes, I like entertaining. It helps me as a person, an individual, to get rid of my ego. If I get rid of the ego on stage, then the problem ceases to exist when I have left there.' Mick Jagger.

Andrew Oldham departed for good, and they were left to their own devices for the first time.

The frantic touring had ceased for a time, and the Rolling Stones were able to concentrate more on their music. After the mixed reception which met *Their Satanic Majesties Request* they bounced right back with the excellent, rip-roaring *Jumpin' Jack Flash*, released in May 1968. The promotional film for this disc was so successful that it prompted the Stones to produce and star in a television extravaganza—The Rolling

PAINT IT BLACK

Stones' Rock and Roll Circus. Directed by Michael Lindsay-Hogg, the spectacular included stars like John Lennon and Yoko Ono, Eric Clapton and Marianne Faithfull.

The release of what has been called 'one of the greatest rock 'n' roll albums of the sixties', *Beggar's Banquet*, should have completed a very successful year. Unfortunately these events were overshadowed by the banning, in America, of the single *Street Fighting Man*, numerous drug raids, and Brian Jones' trial and conviction on yet another charge of possessing dangerous drugs. Even *Beggar's Banquet* was only released after a great deal of trouble and

In 1976 the Rolling Stones toured Europe, taking in eleven countries over three months. Tickets for their London concerts at Earls Court were in such demand that they increased the number of nights there from three to six.

argument over the proposed record sleeve—a graffitied lavatory wall—which Decca Records refused to have anything to do with. The battle between Decca and the Stones raged for five months, until the cover was eventually changed. *Beggar's Banquet* was released in December; the Rock and Roll Circus was yet to be completed.

A great many changes were taking place, the first of which was the replacement of Andrew Oldham by Jimmy Miller as producer of the Stones' records. Miller had made his name

LET IT BLEED

producing people like the Spencer Davis Group—the Stones could be sure that he would work with them to produce the kind of sound that they wanted. *Jumpin' Jack Flash* and *Beggar's Banquet* were the first in a long line of successful productions. They were also ventures in which Brian Jones took little part. For some time, Jones had felt that his own musical tastes and ideas were travelling in a different direction to those of the remainder of the group. He had been the motivation behind the use of electronic instruments on *Their Satanic Majesties Request*, and he wanted to concentrate on that kind of music.

The years of touring had changed Brian Jones. He had always found it difficult to cope with the natural assumption that Mick Jagger was the group leader; and according to the rest of the Stones, he was unable to relate simultaneously to them; there were consequently periods of friction. His insecurity, coupled with general lack of interest in the musical direction of the Rolling Stones, meant that he contributed very little to the current projects. Drugs had changed him: he

The 1976 tour was their first visit to Europe for three years, and it was hailed as a wild success.

had become very frail, both physically and mentally. Matters came to a head at the beginning of June 1969, when Brian Jones quit the Rolling Stones. He resigned after a meeting with the others decided that it would be best if he left to concentrate on his own musical direction, leaving the Stones to concentrate on theirs. Shortly afterwards, the Stones took on a new guitarist, Mick Taylor, who came to them from the blues-orientated John Mayall group.

The Stones now launched themselves into a wave of activity, commencing with a free concert in Hyde Park, arranged for 5 July. Two nights before the concert, and just three weeks after his departure from the group, Brian Jones was pulled from the bottom of his swimming pool. He was unconscious and, despite being given artificial respiration, he died before a doctor could treat him. He was just 27. At the inquest, the coroner recorded 'death due to immersion in fresh water…under the influence of drugs and alcohol. Death by misadventure'. No one ever found out exactly what happened, or why.

Shocked by the news, the Stones nevertheless decided to go ahead with the Hyde Park concert—they felt that Brian Jones would have wished it.

GIMME SHELTER

The Rolling Stones' fans are generally more orderly than they used to be—in the early days the group could hardly get into the theatre, let alone play a concert!

Dedicated to Jones, the concert attracted over 250,000 people. Mick Jagger read from Shelley's *Adonais*, and released thousands of white butterflies—most of which had not survived their confinement in cardboard boxes. The following day, Jagger left for Australia, where he and Marianne Faithfull were to make the film *Ned Kelly*, and on 10 July 1969 Brian Jones was buried.

Another death was to make the headlines that year—the brutal stabbing and beating of Meredith Hunter at the Altamont Speedway rock concert.

The Stones' first tour of America in two and half years had been particularly successful, and to make it even more memorable, they decided to hold a free concert to thank their fans. Only 48 hours before the start of the concert the location had to be changed and the venue picked was Altamont Speedway, a racing track in California. The concert

19TH NERVOUS BREAKDOWN

Ronnie Wood (seen here with Mick Jagger) joined the group permanently in 1975, and the original Stones have since acknowledged his influence, both in the recording studio, and on the road. He himself enjoys the lack of restrictions and finds the Stones inspiring to play with.

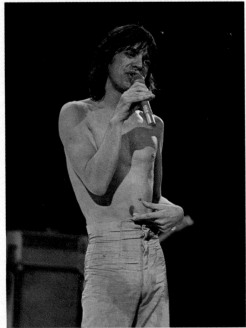

was a disaster. With just a few hours to set up the stage and sound system, arrange facilities for the crowds and some sort of policing for the event, it was inevitable that things should go wrong. To begin with, the site was totally unsuitable, being cold and uncomfor-

START ME UP

table with a general lack of facilities. From the moment the fans started pouring in, dealers were selling contaminated LSD, and this was having an awful effect on the takers. The Stones had been advised to police the event with some local Hell's Angels chapters—for a supply of free alcohol they would undertake crowd control. In the event, they undertook crowd control with excessive zeal.

Artists like Santana, the Grateful Dead and Jefferson Airplane, who appeared

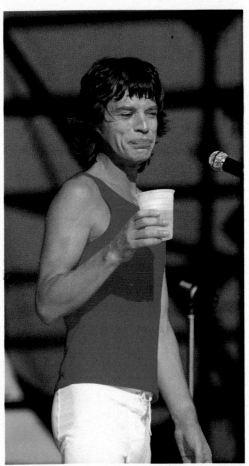

Their 1981 tour of North America, the *first for three years, kicked off in Philadelphia, where they played two shows to an audience of 90,000 each.*

throughout the day, reported later an increasing tension; by the time the Stones came on stage at nightfall, violence among the audience had reached a tremendous pitch. Sparked off by the brutality of the Hell's Angels, this violence culminated in the murder of a young negro, Meredith Hunter. It was suggested at the time that Jagger's antics on stage (the portrayal of Lucifer in *Sympathy for the Devil*, and of the

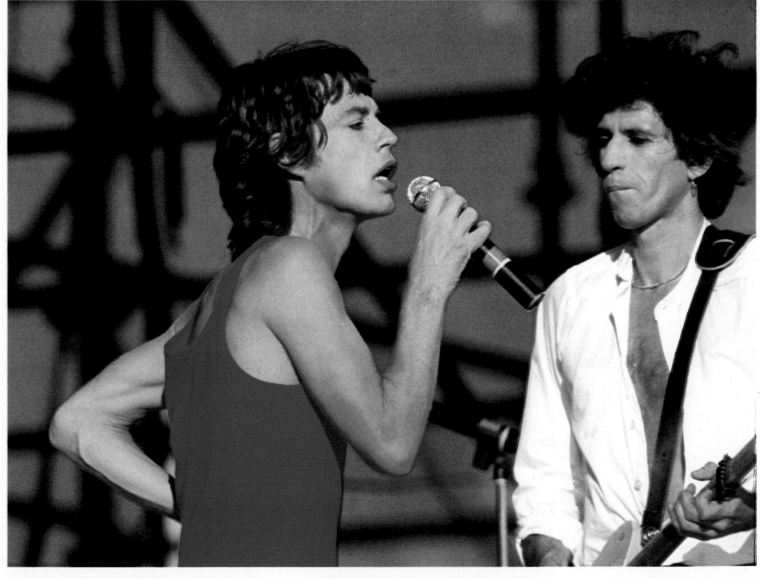

Boston Strangler in *Midnight Rambler*) may have provoked the killing—certainly all concerned admitted that the appallingly bad organisation and lack of facilities had contributed, and that these were the responsibility of the organisers.

The 'swinging Sixties' ended and the Stones rolled into the Seventies with two new hits, the single *Honky Tonk Women*, and the LP *Let It Bleed*, plus various compilation albums, under their belts. Decca finally released *Street Fighting Man* in England, two years after its release in America and just two weeks before the Stones' contract with Decca expired. At about the same time, their association with Allen Klein was brought to an abrupt halt. It was not until March 1971, however, that the Stones, under a contract with Kinney Services Incorporated, were able to release records on a newly-created label—Rolling Stones Records. (EMI took over the licence of Rolling Stones Records in February 1977.)

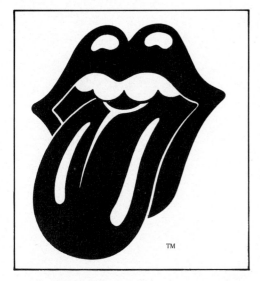

The famous 'lapping tongue' symbol above *became the trademark for Rolling Stones Records in 1971. Overleaf The specially-constructed stage at Philadelphia's John F Kennedy Stadium measured 50 feet high and 200 feet wide, and was flanked by stylish representations of a racing car and guitar on one side, and a pink and blue US flag on the other.*

The first of Mick Jagger's solo movie appearances, as Ned Kelly in the film of the same name, was premièred in 1970. Ned Kelly, a nineteenth century Australian outlaw, was tried and hanged for offences against the state. The film, directed by Tony Richardson, and

Jagger's performance, were not well received by the critics. Nor was Jagger's next film, *Performance*, in which he co-starred with British actor, James Fox. The movie, about a rock superstar and his relationship with a gangster, was

The stadium's car park was filled with *people who camped out overnight for front-row seats—some queued as long as twenty-four hours.*

HAPPY

To get back to the peak of physical *fitness necessary to sing for two-and-a-half hours, and still have the energy to perform* Jumpin' Jack Flash, *Mick Jagger ran several miles daily for a month, played squash and exercised with weights and bar-bells. He continued to train right up until the moment he stepped on stage, and he went 'on the wagon' for three months. At the age of 38, he leaps about with energy that a 20-year-old would envy.*

FOOL TO CRY

premièred in January 1971. Apart from these solo appearances, most of the film material available on the Stones is in the form of concert performances and TV specials; unlike the Beatles, they did not complete a full-length feature film. Even their Rock and Roll Circus remains unscreened.

In March 1971, the Rolling Stones announced they were to live in France from that date—becoming the first rock and roll tax exiles—and just two months

The Stones were unable to play in Canada following Keith Richards' drugs conviction there, so they chose the border town of Buffalo in New York State to entertain their many Canadian fans.

later, in St Tropez, Mick Jagger married Nicaraguan Bianca Perez Morena de Macias. The wedding generated an enormous amount of interest, particularly when Bianca arrived wearing an unusual outfit for a bride. Although she was was dressed in the traditional white, her neckline was slashed almost to the waist! With 'plane-loads of family, friends and, of course, the Press, jetting in, the ceremony could hardly have been anything less than chaotic—much to the happy couple's displeasure—but the riotous reception more than compensated for the earlier fracas.

To many of his fans, Mick Jagger was 'selling-out'. The very idea that he should conform to society's conventions was unthinkable, particularly as he himself

had stated on many occasions that marriage was not for him. His previous relationship, with Marianne Faithfull, had often hit the headlines, and she was finally sued for divorce by her husband, John Dunbar, in 1970, after a four year association with Jagger. Before that, Chrissie Shrimpton, sister of the famous model Jean Shrimpton, had been his steady girlfriend for three years.

Mick Jagger was not the only Stone to marry—Bill Wyman and Charlie Watts had taken the plunge some years before (Bill Wyman was divorced in 1966 after six years of marriage). The Jaggers' daughter, Jade, was born in October 1971; of her Mick Jagger says: 'She's the one thing about it (his marriage to Bianca) that I don't regret.' Mick and Bianca became the darlings of the jet-set, seen in the trendiest nightclubs, like New York's Studio 54, but it soon became apparent that their marriage was breaking down, and Bianca sued for divorce in 1979 after Mick had been living with model Jerry Hall for two years. The divorce was a well-publicised event in which Bianca received an enormous settlement and custody of Jade. Mick Jagger, a doting father, spends as much time as possible with his daughter.

The remaining original Stone, Keith Richards, lived with Anita Pallenberg, former girlfriend of Brian Jones, for eleven years. They parted, and shortly afterwards (in July 1979) Anita Pallenberg's 17-year-old lover shot himself, in the bedroom of the home she had shared with Keith Richards. She was later cleared of any involvement, and she and Richards were reunited for a short time.

Brown Sugar—probably the Stones' single most likely to get people onto the dance floor—was released in April 1971. This was followed just a week later by the release of the controversial *Sticky Fingers* album. Andy Warhol's sleeve design upset many, as did the explicit drug references in the lyrics. A release that month which upset the Stones themselves was an album entitled *Stone Age*, a compilation from Decca which included four tracks then unavailable in Britain. The Stones were particularly irritated by the album's sleeve design—a poor imitation of the graffiti-covered wall artwork for *Beggar's Banquet*, which Decca had censored in 1968. In fact, they

GET OFF OF MY CLOUD

were so annoyed that they took out (at their own expense) an advertisement in every musical paper, disclaiming all knowledge of and responsibility for the album.

The film *Gimme Shelter*, an account of the 1969 North American tour, including the events at Altamont Speedway, was premièred in Britain in July 1971.

The Rolling Stones celebrated their first decade with yet another hit single, *Tumbling Dice*, in May 1972, and the

excellent double album *Exile On Main Street*. They toured North America and Canada in June and July—a tour which had more than its fair share of problems! The scenes of the middle Sixties were repeated when fans rioted, policemen were injured and arrests were made. Mick Jagger and Keith Richards were themselves arrested and released on $3,000 bail after assaulting a photographer at Warwick, Rhode Island. In December, further trouble flared when warrants for the arrest of Keith Richards

The Jagger Strut—he pouts and pleads *and prances, mincing around the vast stage and camping it up for the audience; a mesmerising mixture of gymnastics and ballet.*

and Anita Pallenberg were issued by the French police in connection with drug charges.

As a result of the various drug charges and convictions, the Rolling Stones were banned from entering both Japan and Australia at the beginning of 1973. The Australian authorities relented, however, and the group toured the Far East and Australia from January to the end of

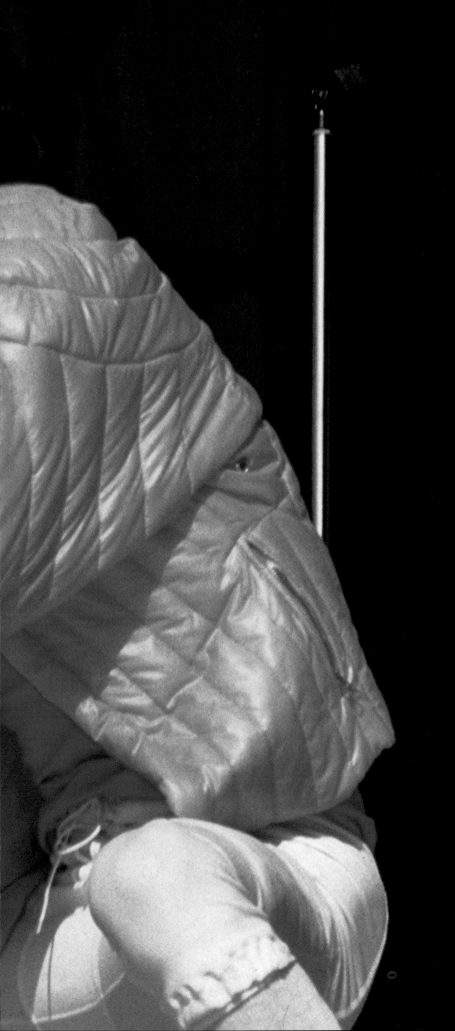
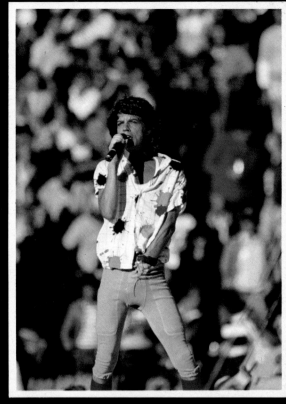

HAVE YOU SEEN YOUR MOTHER, BABY

February, after giving a benefit concert for victims of the Nicaraguan earthquake at the Forum on 18 January, at which they raised more than £200,000. In June, drugs and the Rolling Stones again hit the headlines. Keith Richards, Anita Pallenberg and a friend, Prince Stanislaus Klossowski de Rola, were arrested and charged with possessing cannabis resin; Richards was further charged with possessing a .38 Smith and Wesson revolver without the appropriate firearm licence. The charges against de Rola were dropped, but Keith Richards and Anita Pallenberg were bailed, and in October Richards was fined £205 for the offences, while Anita Pallenberg was given a conditional discharge.

The single *Angie*, released in August 1973, was totally out of keeping with the image of the Stones—yet it became one of their largest-selling records ever. Taken from the LP *Goats Head Soup*, the success of the single almost eclipsed the album, although the banning of one track, *Star Star*, by BBC radio ensured renewed interest!

1974, and the single *It's Only Rock 'N' Roll*, saw the emergence of The Glimmer Twins (alias Mick Jagger and Keith Richards) as record producers. The single also featured Ronnie Wood (soon to become a permanent member of the group) on guitar, together with vocals by David Bowie and additional drums by Kenny Jones. An album of the same name was released in October that year, to mixed reviews. 1974 also saw the departure, in December, of Mick Taylor. After five and a half years with the

STANDING IN THE SHADOW?

Asked why they toured again after three years, Mick Jagger said:'It's good fun. We've always had fun on the road. We still do. We have a good time. That's what it's all about.'

Rolling Stones, he felt he wanted to 'move on and do something new'. His years with the group had added a different dimension to their music, and although it had been difficult for him to take over from Brian Jones without feeling that he was just following in someone else's footsteps, his working relationship with the other Stones was excellent, and his individuality contributed a great deal to their success at the time.

The split came just as the Rolling Stones were preparing for recording sessions in Munich. Rather than rushing into choosing a permanent replacement, however, they decided to use various guest artists on the new album. For their forthcoming tour of the Americas, they chose, as a temporary Stone, Ronnie

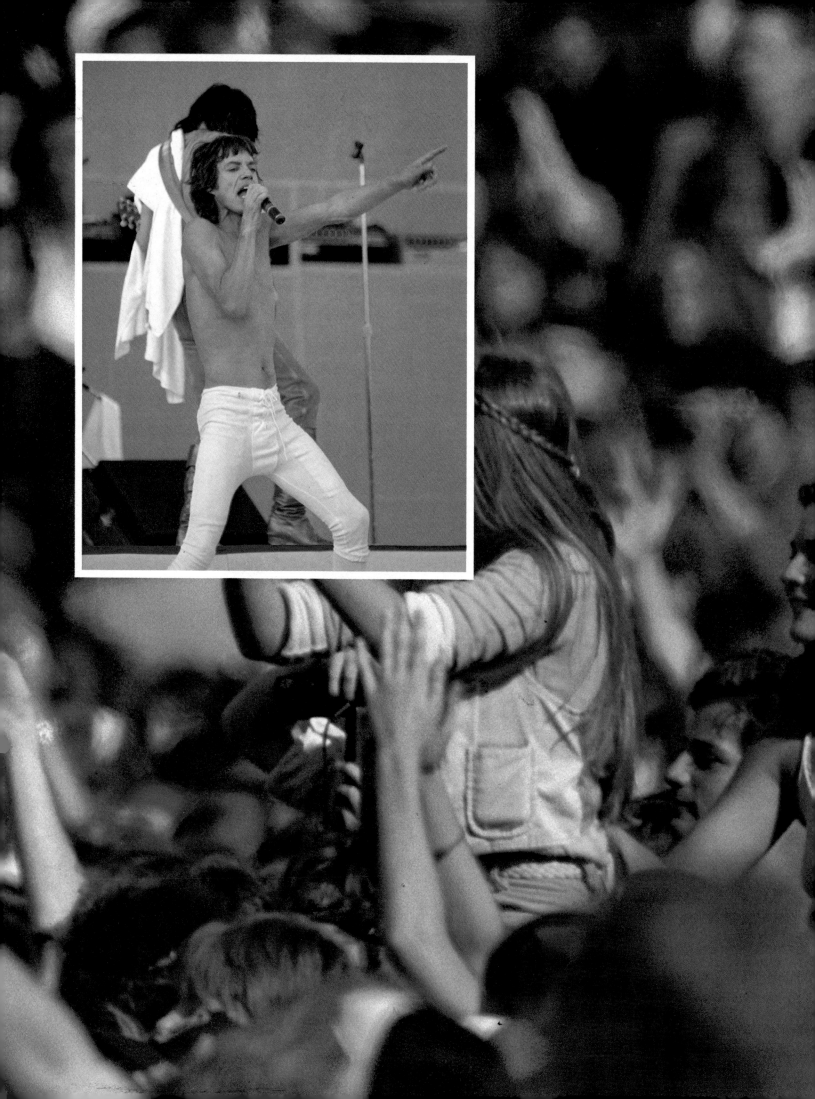

album, *Fool To Cry*, was released as a single on the same day—it was an unqualified success.

In 1977, after years of intensive touring and playing in huge concert halls, the Rolling Stones expressed a desire to play in the more intimate clubs to smaller audiences. One of the first such venues was the El Mocambo Club in Toronto, Canada. Keith Richards was promptly

A ten-minute-long version of Jumpin' Jack Flash *ends when Jagger, finding the enormous stage too small to contain him, swings out over the crowd in the cab of a 'cherrypicker' crane and throws red and white carnations to his fans* far right.

Wood, who was then lead guitarist with The Faces. The tour was so successful that he was offered the position permanently in December that year. His technique, totally different to that of Mick Taylor, takes the Stones back to their original form—a more basic, rhythmic style.

Although *Black and Blue*, the Stones' next major release, was issued well after Ronnie Wood joined the group, it was not until the following album, *Some Girls*, that Wood's influence could be heard. In fact, *Black and Blue* had been recorded between December 1974 and April 1975, but not released until 20 April 1976 when it met with mixed reaction. One of the most uncharacteristic tracks on the

EMOTIONAL RESCUE

arrested by the Canadian Mounties for alleged drug trafficking and, in a separate incident, Anita Pallenberg was charged with possession of hashish and heroin. She was later fined, but Richards chose trial by judge and jury after losing his application to be charged with possession rather than trafficking.

He was found guilty and given a suspended sentence, on condition that

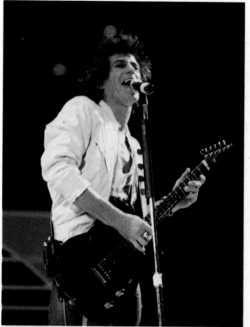

he organised and performed in a concert on behalf of the blind within six months, and continued his treatment for drug addiction. (He kicked the heroin habit after three weeks of treatment.)

The arrest of Richards and Pallenberg was not the only 'incident' that happened during the Rolling Stones' visit to Canada: Mick Jagger's alleged affair with Mrs Margaret Trudeau, wife of the Canadian premier, caused an international scandal and almost toppled the Canadian government! It

The 1981 tour was an unqualified success, particularly financially, with proceeds from film, TV and video rights, souvenir T-shirts, advertising on admission tickets, and earnings from the new best-selling album Tattoo You, *as well as phenomenal ticket sales.*

certainly prompted a temporary (90 day) separation between Premier Trudeau and his wife.

Apart from the release of two albums, *Emotional Rescue* in June 1980, and *Tattoo You* in September 1981, the Rolling Stones went into semi-retirement after their 1978 tour of North America and the Canadian benefit concerts. Then, in September 1981, they embarked upon an American tour as ambitious as anything they had undertaken in the past. Nearly twenty years after their sessions at the Crawdaddy Club, and fifteen years

after the hysteria and riots at the peak of their popularity, they began a three-month programme of concerts in twenty cities across the continent. They played to fans who were not even born when the group formed, to fans who had followed the Stones throughout their career, to the newly-converted, and to those who were veterans of four or five concerts. As one 23-year-old stated:

'They're the greatest rock 'n' roll band in the world. They symbolise rock 'n' roll, a good time and partying.'

At the start of the tour, the Rolling Stones played in a small club in Worcester, Massachusetts, under an assumed name. The secret was leaked, and the club was mobbed by thousands of fans. In scenes reminiscent of the early days, they were banned from appearing in any other of the small clubs they had booked, and on the morning of the first concert, in Philadelphia, a local clergyman appeared on television condemning the lyrics of *Satisfaction* as immoral, just as others had, years before. The adverse publicity had little effect—in Philadelphia alone they played to a crowd of 90,000 on the largest stage ever built for a concert, and during the tour it was estimated that a total audience of three million people saw them; just the ticket sales earned $40 million. Indeed, the tour was so successful that it was extended by almost two weeks.

The 1981 tour of North America has been a triumph for the Rolling Stones—not only have they survived in a profession noted for its impermanence, they have proved that after twenty years they can still claim to be one of the greatest rock and roll bands the world has ever seen.

Acknowledgements: With thanks to Keith Altham Enterprises and Rolling Stones Records for their help.

First published in Great Britain 1982 by Colour Library International Ltd.
© 1982 Illustrations and text: Colour Library International Ltd., New Malden, Surrey, England.
Colour separations by FERCROM, Barcelona, Spain.
Display and text filmsetting by Focus Photoset, London, England.
Printed and bound in Barcelona, Spain by JISA-RIEUSSET & EUROBINDER.
ISBN 0 86283 007 9
COLOUR LIBRARY INTERNATIONAL

DLB 16094